After Rain

ALSO BY CAROLYN HUNTER

Writing:
Photographic Memory Camera

Music:
Lovelight
Heartstring Hunters
Seeds with Wings

after rain

poems and stories by
Carolyn Hunter

illustrated by
Jessica Bernstein

Beehive Media
Boulder, Colorado

FIRST EDITION

*For Daniel, Hemingway, Dixie
and my Colorado family.*

In loving memory of Tyrone.

I am beyond sound and sight,

I cannot be touched,

I am She who dwells behind the veil of matter.

They ask if I exist

And I answer that I do

and I do not;

but at the end of cycles and seasons,

which some name Death

but those who have lifted my veil name Life,

on the shores of the Sea of Time you will find me,

my head turned to the wind,

walking by the waves of the eons and waiting,

for your coming and your going.

Excerpt from "The Charge of Arianrhod"

CONTENTS

These poems reflect my journey into a new realm. From pandemic to pregnancy, death to rebirth. The coming together of my marriage, the honoring and grieving of my maiden self, and the birth of a mother. The experiencing and feeling, scribbling, doubting, and persevering – all are pitter-patter on the cold hard ground. This book is what lies beyond the clearing.

BECOMING

In the becoming she had time to dream
sleep filled nights
she built a garden
watched purple and yellow things grow from the earth
for the first time
asked herself why chickens laid so many eggs
for the first time
picked seeds from flowers' center and chewed them up

her world was quiet

In the becoming she barely wrote
she learned to feel things and love her animals
she stood on her land and learned where North, South,
East and West stood back
for the first time

In the becoming
she let others believe what they wanted about her
she let her belly get soft and her breasts grow round
fingers stained with pollen
for the first time

In the becoming
numbing no longer served her and so she sat
still
like the northern star
sparkling under the haze
of the fires
and the chemicals
and the threats of civil war
and
still
she breathed

WE WERE DANCING

we were dancing beneath the sky light
moon beams falling on our cheeks
when the winds shifted

horses ran free
farmers gathered livestock
people ran

we were spinning in circles in the soft grass
dizzy with belly laughs
when the winds shifted

homes were eaten
musicians gathered their guitars
and their children

we were visiting our sister in another state
strolling the newborn on the sidewalk
when the winds shifted

neighbors were called
to help find the kitten
to go in top drawers
for vows and letters
that cannot be rewritten

we were finding our way again
with masks and distance and borders
when the winds shifted

ASHEVILLE

I dream of blueberry scones
and when I add banana
I am Asheville
a cafe and a braid
the future
or another life
twice-baked before
in the heat of Appalachia
a dream in a heart of something more
laid to rest on the cooling racks
of frozen eastern driveways and ponds
a shop on a hill
the smoky mountains
a song beneath a river
a girl in a party dress
lost among the Spanish moss

5

SECRET HEARTS

are we not our secret hearts?
will I perish never knowing the reckless leap of resolution
it will take to not abandon myself?
our own desire,
a sinking ship
from which we push and shove our way to the half-life
boats of which there are not enough

must I walk through life a tourist?
the wine forever smelling like someone else's history?
might I then just rather be a memory you lie with forever
than a body you've grown indifferent to?
the courage it must take to allow oneself more than
the feasting off memories and dreams

to be one so convicted
in her belief in life,
she screams down the alleyways
Life chose me to believe in!
LIFE CHOSE ME TO BELIEVE IN!

TURMERIC & CINNAMON

they want to hear the story of how we met

but we're all cinnamon and turmeric meeting in corners
of cupboards

we're all live music that drifts down the block from a
rowdy bar

somewhere on the east coast

a story our children might never understand

DECEMBER

Write one haiku a day for a year.
That was the challenge, and this is what came out.

an orange, a clove
mulled wine and hot chocolate
a birthday, a friend

bacon in a pan
can't hide the stench of
misunderstanding

owls and earthworms
split the deck and then again
a friendship at ease

a gentle pleasure
to find peace in a story
in old softened wood

sage the rented rooms
of opening and regret
breathe in life's promise

growling at nothing
youth on a bender
howling at the moon

seeking rooted warmth
she lays in the garden bed
where lost things blossom

the gentlest of words
two hands on my warm belly
delights of old love

bristles of knowing
windswept clouds over the moon
surely life will come

a single tear fell
the night of winter's solstice
sweet intransigence

hawk eyes at sunrise
soaring above mountain grass
warm breeze from the east

wildfires blowin'
one hundred miles per hour
creatures huddle in

red wine and champagne
lasagna and crème brûlée
new years eve, my love

KANSAS

I dream the lucid dream of revolving bird cages
tilted and golden
swirling with birds inside
shadows of birds flying out
I return every time I close my eyes
I force myself to wake and stare at the hotel alarm clock
frightened
the room a black abyss
in the morning the grave tender trudges gently over the
greenery
large willows hang their heavy green leaves
wheat fields as far as the eye can see
a police car sits at the edge of the parking lot

STAFFORD, VIRGINIA

past the trailer park and the auto shop
through the last stretch of farms and homes on the hill
I'd like to go back where the walls move and the tables
fold and roll
blue doors, exit signs, water fountains, duckling lines
almost never teased
but for having big teeth and being the teacher's pet
teeth the boys ask to lick now
almost never kicked out
but for church giggles in the pledge of allegiance
standing in the hallway alone
pretending I had somewhere to go
one nation under the gods
of Roald Dahl and Judy Blume, Shel Silverstein
and the art teacher with the golden Egyptian hieroglyphs
before I lied and bled
there was a fair
books appeared out of nowhere and stayed for a week
and on Monday the stage was just a stage
like a one-night stand that doesn't leave you empty
you have a colorful new story and a bookmark
now I ask too much of books
make me bigger, stronger, richer, smarter
make me an author
make me succeed
and I ask too much of men
make me safer, warmer, more powerful, more loved
make me a mother
make me succeed
I'd like to go back where the walls move and the tables
fold and roll
past the trailer park and the auto shop
through the last stretch of farms and homes on the hill

JANUARY

seatbelts on airplanes
high above the pacific
no dry land in sight

the birds come to bathe
he sweeps the plumerias
morning rooster crows

poi and fried reef fish
strawberry beet jam basil
macadamia butter

three nights in the hospital
I dreamt of New York
I dreamt of crisp days

WAITING IN LINE

for Rachel

some cities tap on your soul, she said and leaned in

New Orleans does that...

tap tap tap

13

MANY-FACED GOD

I close my eyes and face the side of the room with the boarded-up window.

On nights like this I serve the many-faced God.

I take your mask from the shelf.

I am at a strange socially distanced party, on your lap, and you say, "When I met you...you were around 100?...and now you're what...110?"

I feel the weight of your words. I lean in.

"I've gained ten pounds since the start of winter. Or quarantine. Or since my partner moved back."

"I like it," I say. "I like the curves and the softness."

"I could stand to gain a few pounds back then." I continue, repeating something my best friend said to me during week 4.

You shake your head. "Nahh."

Like, "Nahh you really couldn't stand those pounds."

You are the most cruel. Most capable of inflicting pain. Your face, a reflection, my rejection and loss of self.

When I am at my worst, I wear you.

FEBRUARY

snowshoeing in high country
towering green pines
newspapers and blue eyes

> *burrowed deep in white*
> *she falls into the snowpack*
> *a fall that will last all year*

> *protecting my dreams*
> *I wear grief I wear*
> *rings across my throat*

ISOLATION

i was building a mattress for us inside of a tent that you said you wanted to camp in and i took pads from inside little sleeping pods from inside of a boat or maybe a bus, to make it comfier, but you didn't come, you actually went with my friend Samantha from middle school, we always had the same boyfriends, and you were bald one moment, then had a clean cut haircut the next, it was all very confusing, and I said something to Samantha like "haha our taste in men" but then I realized that maybe he didn't tell her that he was originally coming there for me, maybe she was very confused by that, i laughed, but this time when i sent you a nude you responded in full sentences and I sank into you like you opened an umbrella in the rain even though the doorman called me Cassandra

DEFEAT

my dreams are dying

and I know new ones will take their place

that's how life is
you love the life you live
and everything that led you to it

but my dreams are dying

and I wasn't prepared for this defeat

a girl who dreams big
must sleep big
I told my lover
jokingly

but my dreams are dying
and all I can do now

is weep

TAKE ME TO THE VINEYARD

for Daniel

take me to the vineyard
lay me beneath the vine
sing to me of children
sing what's on your mind
mine the clay beneath the earth
mine is yours in death in birth

take me to the vineyard
sow me seeds of galleries
sing to me of fallen leaves
of art and music and pottery
mine the clay beneath the earth
mine is yours in death in birth

pour the wine
on dusty roads
in scarlet trees
beneath the vine

sing to the child
on porch swings
in golden leaves
beneath the vine

hold your mother
on cold days
in rolling hills
beneath the vine

INTO THE SILENCE

in a house in a canyon
we once had nothing but a bed
and before the refrigerator sang
we fell into
the silence like the midnight sky
the snow fell
and we ran madly from shack to shack
hair flying wildly in the wind
slippers slipping on ice and mud
tangled up in heaters and extension cords
we rolled the bins and cursed the gods
for knocking us down again and again
like the many mailboxes
who could also never win
we screamed at the dogs
for chasing the bears
for stealing the trash
and the dogs screamed back
and all of us screamed
into
the silence like the northern sky

MARCH

geese on glass and snow
ice circled by water's edge
moonlit night we walk

oh euphoria
oh to feel like this always
stay like this always

tiny bean below
the feeling of a full tide
a full moon and more

you are safe you are
healthy you are loved you are
wanted you are who you are

each day a wanting
a watching and a waiting
I protect you from the world

the void disappears
as I turn and think of you
all is here and more

one hand on belly
daddy's here daddy's here
eyes closed lost in thought

roadkill, dead racoon
shiver at our deadly world
our roads and fast cars

the perfect burger
no lettuce or tomato
no onion, cheese please

22

a weekend away
asleep below burning stars
cows mew in the night

learning to let go
I am learning to let go
god above, hold me

don't worry my love
I do enough of such things
be the water's touch

FORGIVENESS COMES

I drew an angel card and it said Children. And quickly after, you came. In the beginning, the morning was always my favorite time. Belly empty of food, I would lay flat and could feel you as your own small unit, a little shellfish or cocoon whole unto yourself, but buried deep inside me. I would swim in the pool and press against the concrete edges, there I could also feel you like this, mine, but your own. I would wade in the shallows and press my belly lightly against the ocean floor. I could feel you then too, against me, and against the world. Like nothing I've ever felt before. When you were a blueberry, I wished for you to become a strawberry. And when you were a strawberry, I wished for you to become a pineapple. And on and on.

But you have always been a mermaid, a mystery.

And because of you I say...

Forgiveness comes when there is no more room for hurt or hate.
When love is too great and purpose is found
in the rivulets of life to the ocean.
Forgiveness comes with a small growing thing.
Where the soil must be full of rain and love and big sighs.
Forgiveness comes when you grow bigger than your need to be right.

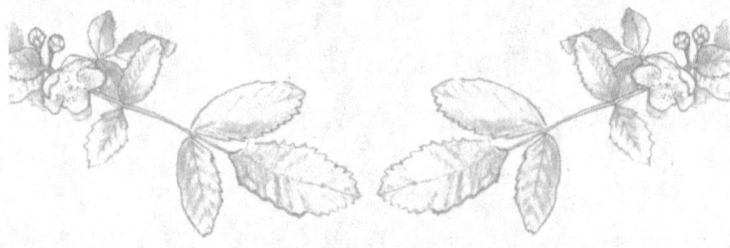

HOW CAN I GIVE A POEM

how can I give a poem
I give kisses and snuggles
my beauty my spirit
these lines
crevices of immunity
these words
corners of my being
cracks in my knowing
gusts of love that sweep through my bones
with urgency
made permanent
through ink alone
how can I give a poem
I give warmth and caressing
my nights
my nourishment
my joys my sorrows
my mouth
my tongue
these words
footprints of
a lone path
a soul's path
offshoots of wonder
backroads of despair
how can I give a poem
my toes on your ankles
our thighs interwoven
my windows and dawns
these lines
chemical interruptions
screams of generations
flustered butterflies
that gust through and find themselves
out of my fingertips
how can I give a poem

DOWN THE HILL

I wait in the corner of the yard down the hill
for the little girl to come
and pretend to be a girl sitting in a tree
we watch the tire swing in the aftermath of her passing
and the sun sparkles on the leaves
she's waited all day to come
and pretend to be a girl reading in a tree
for whom God and Life has chosen for this very moment
she sits and speaks in all her glory
and pretends to be a girl who talks to trees
I wish I could tell her
that she is
oh she is!
she is talking to me

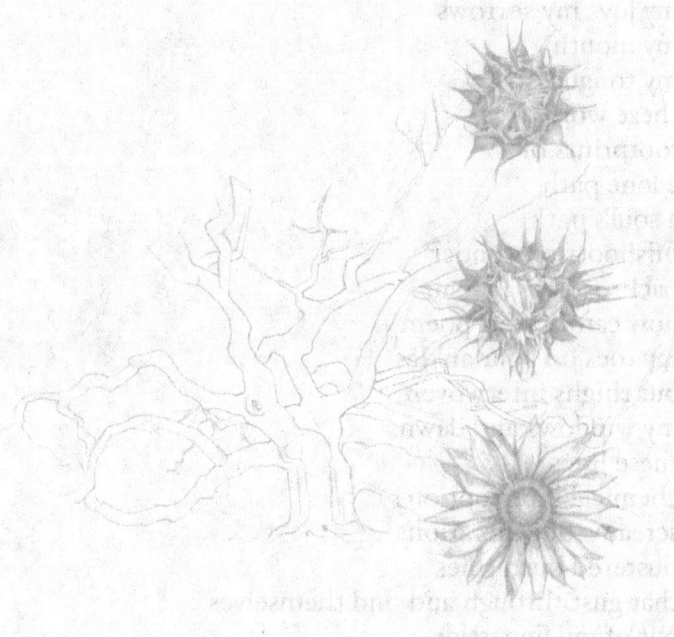

APRIL

burgers in bathtubs
beyond all air mattress threats
I lick my fingers

> *float down the Yukon*
> *my ocean in your canoe*
> *your dream before mine*

> *the art of worry*
> *a fine collection of grit*
> *catch pull reflect sift release*

like dogs and dreaming
how quickly I have become
a mother, to you

all great things begin
whiskers and whiskey and wind
with whimsical wuhs

THE KITTEN & MY HEART

to all those we leave behind
and journey onward without

lying there with her in the empty house
breath on breath
we said goodbye
she clung to me
the last living thing in the house
no furniture but a small black couch
we're moving to the city, I tell her
you won't like it there

her first spring
and me
shaking with nerves
I let her roam free
so many things to be afraid of up here
lions and hawks
bear and fox

but you were always clever
moving through the grass
learning the land
up the pine trees
and in the wood pile out front
spending your days
on the warmth of the roof
flat and hot in the afternoon

one winter
you were snowed out for days
what went through your mind
when you woke up
snowed inside?
we thought you had been eaten

but you returned to us one night
rubbing up against the red door
making us beg for you
come back inside

in the neighbors' broke down car you would hide
but you'd always return
with a mole, with a mouse
covered in oil, we had you
clawing out of the clawfoot tub,
running like a wet rat through the house

I will miss you
my kitten
I miss you now
the feel of your spine
rising with the touch of my hands
your soft whiskers
tickling my cheeks
catching glimpses of you in the trees
your cross-eyed gaze
in small soft balls of gray
your purring and kneading
softening my nerves

my kitten, my heart,
Sparrow

WITNESS

if you rubbed my belly a thousand times
said hello and goodbye
it would never be enough

if you waited for hours
with both hands and baited breath
it would never be enough

for there are more
when you walk away
and who is there to feel them but me

is that enough

I cannot beg for the witness

I can only hold space for the miracle

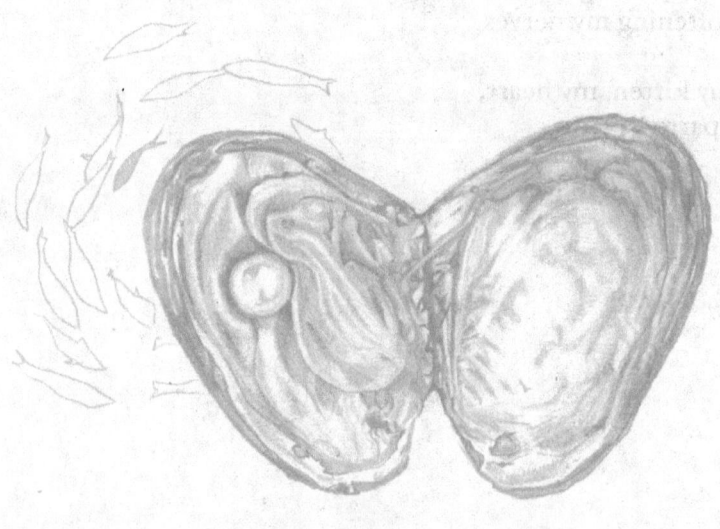

MAY

high meadow valley
breathe and watch my family
ponderosa pines

I dream and then wake
a dream of the yellow cake
with the white icing

full belly circles
jojoba and verbana
glance my reflection

it's never as good
as they say it should be here
and yet here I am

is nothing easy?
am I meant to be alone?
water from the sea

water from the sea
a gift in a Sprite bottle
the sea, the dead sea

I bathe my hands in
the minerals and the grit
flowing like a prayer

is it me who wrongs?
who needs to be given all
and work for nothing?

MARRIAGE

marriage is a haunted house
costumed and disillusioned, secret and enchanted

marriage is a list of instructions
for assembly and use
one spoon of sugar, fan on low, forks up in the dishwash-
er, orange pants do not dry

marriage is a question
where are my scissors, where is my tape measurer, where
are my nail clippers, where have you been

marriage is an answer
of course, always, yes, I'll be there, I love you too

marriage is a grandfather clock

is time

is rain

a magnet

a bath drain

God's hands

a family

a sailboat

a job

an oil painting

a home

an embrace

a feat

a failure

a triumph

fate

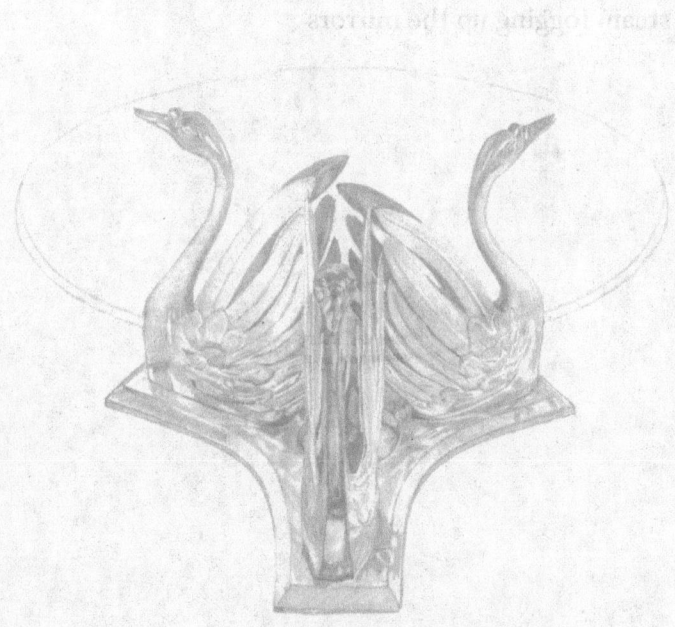

MORNING GAZE

for Daniel

If I could paint you to remember
I'd paint you in the early morning shower
left hand across your waist
right hand to the indent in your chest above your heart
like paws, like mitts
hunched slightly, still wrapped in sleep
and the burning water cascades down
toe hair running toward the drain
steadfast and unbothered
chin lowered
blueberry eyes look up at me
wet and sparkling
knee knocked
feet splayed
steam fogging up the mirrors

JUNE

white and blue linen
dull on the wheel of always
I turn and I yearn

a great endeavor
a rebellion of slowness
of silence and love

I am your mother
I am your sanctuary
until thanksgiving

breathe underwater
my husband wants this of me
to be unafraid

ASHBURY HEIGHTS

for Rachel

my friend she is the wind
and if I am a forest
she is Ashbury Heights
but only in its prime
she is freedom
and I am a bookshelf
I fly on her wings
and she rests in me
the bedside lamp lights up a book of longing
and she lights up a book in me
my friend she is the wind
a path
so much I want my child to be
running naked through the starry trees
my friend, my child
like sand, like dreams
you can't hold on
to anything

SEAL BIRD

Little seal bird, we like to go camping on the weekends.
We set up a big tent and stare up at the clouds and the
blue skies and the pines that wave above us.
Sometimes it gets windy at night and it feels like you're
on a great ship out at sea.
Then the birds signal morning with their songs and
chirps and banter and screeches.
This is my favorite part. Waking to the birds with you in
my belly pressed against the backside of your daddy. You
are right in the middle, right where you should be.

I work most days, and wash all of your things. I yearn to
dry everything of yours in the sun, so I lay them across
backyard chairs and promise myself I'll hang a line. I
wonder why I don't feel the same about mine.

When I tell him you are giving me big rolls, he tells me
you are getting excited for all your new clothes and toys.
I laugh, and long to birth you right into a soft nest of
grass in the shining sun.

Little seal bird, it is getting harder to breathe, and easier
to live.

MYSELF AS MUCH

the colored rings are stacked, the books lined neatly on
the shelves
each small sleeper washed and folded, organized by size
and softness
white woven baskets full of toys await your small hands
and mouth

I hope I love you as much
as each page is chewed and ripped, each pastel wooden
ring scattered and lost
I hope I love myself as much

the doula is chosen, the midwives are ready,
classes taken, books read
my bag is packed with coconut water and candles and
prayers

I hope I love you as much
when you decide in your own unstoppable way, how to
come through me and into this world
I hope I love myself as much

maternity leave plans are made, daycare waitlists know
you by both possible names
I hope I love you as much
when I find that I want to go back to work early, or
worse, never want to leave your side again
I hope I love myself as much

I love everything in its place
and your perfect cloth diapers will be stained

I hope I love you as much
I hope I love myself as much

so I let your daddy's crumbs fall into the sheets
and with my mascara on, try to fall asleep
I'd like to prepare for marriage as much as the wedding
the care and keeping of you as much as the passage

but maybe that is just another illusion
as if I could ever prepare for such a thing
as if I could ask you to simply look at the perfectly
stacked pastel wooden rings

JULY

profound fluttering
squirming of a child
beneath skin and bone

      peace of a closed door
      a humming fan at midday
      cool sheet, close the blinds

            envision future
            portrait of a traveler
            mother and child

            far away from here
            I hold a small hand
            and eat the food off the street

courage to seek joy
to lie down and rest when needed
to be an artist

      I want you to stay
      you will find him in the hills
      and me in my room

      my small room of words
      chained together move mountains
      ones you do not climb

I see wonderous things
when I close my eyes midday
In the cool dark room

I see wonderous things
when I sip morning coffee
liquid unburnt hope

I want my baby
want December in August
want the next best thing

what happened to me
am I even a snowflake
to land upon God

to make it matter
but matter is never made
nor is it destroyed

41

STRANGERS

It's not too late for us to be strangers again.
I stomached it last night between mouthfuls of tortellini
gone cold in uncomfortable conversation.
And again this morning, in between the anxiousness and
the weightlessness.
I want to jump for the eraser.
But I let it sit beside me.
The strangeness that is.
Try not to make it right.
Try not to make it right.
I tell myself.
And just when I think I can't take it.
The strangeness that is.
Like a woman suffering from Alzheimer's who hears a
song and remembers,
I see the black silhouettes against the orange rocks of the
canyon.
Against the asphalt.
And then the mountain.
Flashes of the engine. Two helmets, my hoodie flapping
wildly behind us like Amelia Earhart in flight.
And I remember.
Like riding a bike perhaps.
But in a clawfoot tub filled with only water.
Soap only making things stickier in the stillness.
Our history never leaves us.
And still we must meet.

DIXIE GYPSY JANGLE

remember when we snuck into the trailer park pool after
hours and we tied Dixie to a table near camp no dogs al-
lowed and we dove in and I crawled all over you wet on
wet but she dragged the picnic table down the path so
we let her off and she jumped in and we thought if we
got caught oh well somewhere in Indiana and we laughed
and laughed and I watched her doggy paddle to you in the
deep end thinking I was so lucky you were a rule breaker
because two followers just wouldn't have any fun and only
when we tired all three of us walked back to the bus in the
gravel spot by the missing table under the cocoon of the
midwestern sky

FIREFLIES

she speaks until she's forced to breathe
he falls asleep anytime he reads
fireflies and motorcycle rides
he bites the air she hunts the sky

SUMMER OF LOVE

salvage
the moss and the summer
your words into a lone wolf stew
a little more
savage
with each
reuse

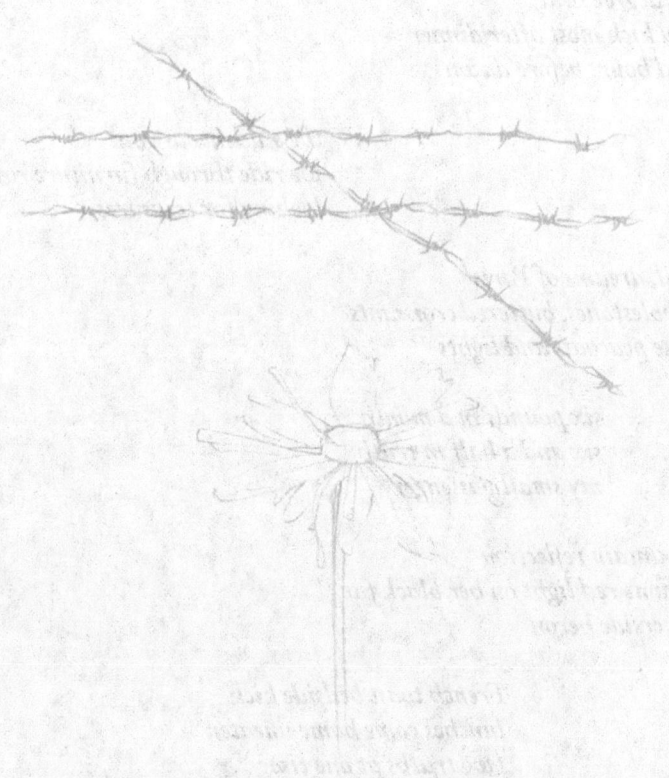

AUGUST

underwater warmth
quiet in the chlorine lane
stillness underworld

        light the battalion
        I have come for playfulness
        Angel tarot card

80-degree heat
you kick most after dinner
and hours before dawn

                the students are out
                we ride through furniture row
                looking for treasures

still, dreams of Paris
cobblestones, buttered croissants
blue peacoats and lights

        six pounds in a month
        six and a half in truth
        my small passenger

mountain reflection
dawn's red light on her black fur
riverside heron

        French toast bedside kick
        lunches come home uneaten
        two truths at one time

what are my branches
that must be cut away from
my ripening fruit

46

LATE SUMMER

When you are gone I take in the umbrella
and cry over the nursery

pregnancy is an ocean
a prickly vine, late summer squash

I wish to hold the seashell to your ear
the longing, also a gift

my love drives through the night
and wear out the tires of life

I watch the cherry tomatoes
fall to the grass
and feel sad I couldn't keep up

BY THE RIVER

soft and round in the heat of the afternoon
an aquarium lightshow
first spotted on the rotted log
falls across my inner thigh
I splash cold water between my legs
not sure where to go from here
but if all rivers lead to the ocean
then I can give myself grace
I hop on my bike and head down the gravel path
dogs running beside me
not a thing in sight
but a light blue Cadillac half eaten by the forest
tiny yellow leaves twinkle in the ache of autumn
I find shade and lay flat, eyes closed
your gentle snores like coyotes in the darkness

ROCKING CHAIR POETRY

we all love to swing back and forth
back and forth
back and forth
the same somatic kind of love
back and forth
that brought you into this world
will rock you back to the womb ocean of your primordial
dreams
isn't it all the same
and we're all just dreaming
we all love to sway
side to side
the universal dance to all that is good and strange and
alive
side to side
the same dance that kept us whole enough, gave us spirit
enough to imagine you to thrive
will sway you out of your most terrifying nightmares and
seduce you back to the beauty of earth
hips on a walk, up a mountain, to a tune in the kitchen
we will cradle your small head like all the dancers who
ever dipped their partners before us
side to side
back and forth
ever moving
never still
side to side
back and forth
back and forth
don't we all love to dream

SEPTEMBER

baby manchild
freakout nursery blue temper
the wind in my hair

oh my aching back
give me pleasure and relief
one body two months

sag paneer on blues
samosa and mint chutney
building a nursery

compromise, anger
codependent, resentment
alone in my thoughts

my nursery meltdown
a newborn fashion crisis
repeating patterns

twenty-seven pounds
autumnal melancholy
and blissful secrets

my wolves want to run
but I can only walk slow
what have humans done

November she calls
for record players and milk
sweet affirmations

maybe I've lost it
she's still by the campfire
beside woodland dreams

I want my baby
I want a house in Asheville
I couldn't do it

rocking chair glory
excavating the hunger
drowning in the past

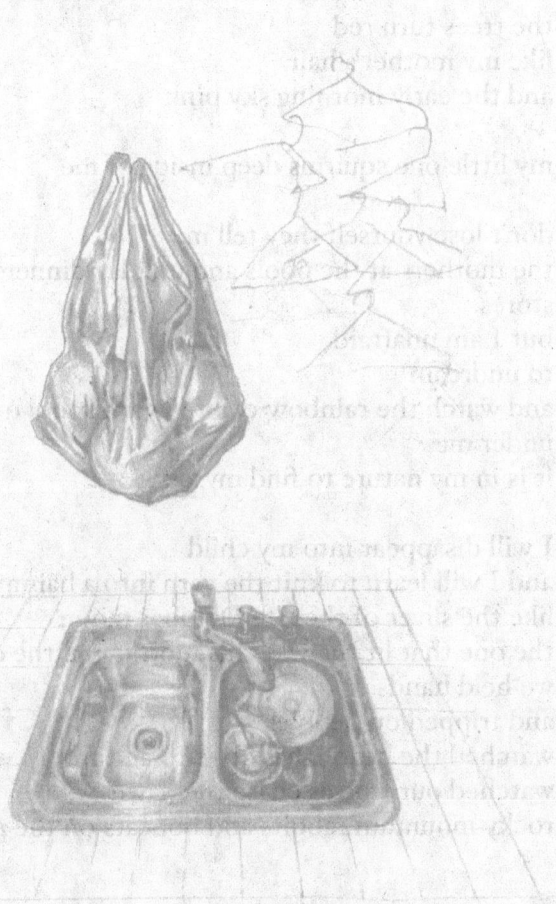

UNDREAMING

October is near
melancholy floats in and hides the sun
the birds fly above
and another year has passed

the trees turn red
like my mother's hair
and the early morning sky pink

my little one squirms deep inside of me

don't lose yourself they tell me
the mothers at the pools and holiday dinners and grocery
stores
but I am unafraid
to undream
and watch the rainbow-colored yarn spool out from
under me
it is in my nature to find myself

I will disappear into my child
and I will learn to knit the yarn into a hammock
like the sliver of the late October moon
the one that lit the way this morning in the darkness as
we held hands
and tripped on pebbles
watched the headlights drive to and fro
watched our wolves chase the dawn
rocky mountain rabbits and bobcats on the ridge

OCTOBER

lovechild yearning
inside me she lies afloat
angel of spirit

          strong and resilient
          temple body of the night
          walking into light

     life in slow motion
     everything in its right place
     waiting for lightning

Volkswagen onward
remembered soliloquy
midwestern forest

BEAT OF THE BONES

I find myself here
each October
heart newly flustered
in a vast yard
ghostly parts of me
tortured, shackled
wanting only death
"Put me out of my misery!" they cry
as I drag them into each new day
if only I could sort out
the living and the dead
and march to the beat of
the bones
might I then fly in the wind
that sings of Berlin
of classical music
and salt on my eyelashes

AUBREY

She was a strange girl. Tall for a girl of 13. She had a gait about her. A walk like she might fall forward. She wore a necklace with a black leather cord and a silver pendant in the shape of a circle with a star in the middle. It wasn't the cross. It was Wicca. And Wicca was the devil in my town.

One day, Aubrey bled through her white pants and walked right out of our classroom with her head held high and a sweater half tied around her waist. It was 7th grade science class, and I can still see her walking out the door like it was yesterday.

I glance at my new book on the dining room table. *Wicca: A Comprehensive Guide to the Old Religion in the Modern World* by Vivianne Crowley.

I think about Aubrey.
Her books and her blood and her pendant. Her velvet pants and white gloves and long coat. Her acne, and body odor and oiled hair. The butt of our jokes, the outcast.

I open my book.

"I am She who dwells behind the veil of matter."

Witch we called her. Witch we pointed and laughed. Witch we whispered as we moved our trays away from hers in the cafeteria. She cast a spell out to all of us and laughed. She had a marvelous laugh. Deep and throaty like someone who had nothing to lose and who had everything at the same time.

"I am beyond sound and sight, I am She who dwells behind the veil of matter."

When she spoke, she had a slightly odd English accent to her like she had grown up watching only medieval movies. I liked when she read out loud in class because she was an excellent reader. She was always reading. I imagine her with her nose in a book at her desk or returning to our classroom in a pair of our school's canary blue gym shorts.

"I am beyond sound and sight,
I cannot be touched,
I am She who dwells behind the veil of matter."

I wish now I had been friends with her. But she was untouchable. She had more blood, more books, more thoughts. She was brave in an impossible place. I look up the meaning of Aubrey because I want to use a pseudonym for her but nothing seems to fit.
"Aubrey: From a Norman French form of the Germanic name Alberic, composed of alb, meaning "elf, supernatural being" and ric, meaning "power" and taken to mean "ruler of elves"

I stare at my book on my table *Wicca: A Comprehensive Guide to the Old Religion in the Modern World.*

"I am beyond sound and sight,
I cannot be touched,
I am She who dwells behind the veil of matter.
They ask if I exist
and I answer that I do
and I do not;
but at the end of cycles and seasons,
which some name Death
but those who have lifted my veil name Life,
on the shores of the Sea of Time you will find me,
my head turned to the wind,
walking by the waves of the aeons and waiting,
for your coming and your going."

*Excerpt from "The Charge of Arianrhod"

56

HALLOWS

feed the autumnal hunger and
cast a spell into the starry night
a spell of courage for the druid inside
the veil is thin and the vampiric self
is overfed
unhook echoes of espionage
dim the red light made brighter by the
lusty onlooker
what could you become, severed from
the gaze of ghosts across the land?
your cauldron is leaking *joie de vivre*
and you must make
your world here again
for spirit, for now, for all that is to come
carve a lantern with a devilish grin to light
the path
build a scarecrow and let no one feast upon
the scraps

ANY DAY NOW

I want to give you the moss
and the fallen acorns beneath the large oak tree
want to give you dirt covered hands
and satisfaction as whole pieces break free

pumpkins and witches and goblins
star covered skies, dark streets with wanderers and
ghouls
want to give you your father's eyes
the very same ones that I fell through

and when you think of fall
I hope you think of your nana
bright red hair that turns to blonde
playing pickleball in the Florida sun

and when you think of fall
I hope you think of your papa
marrying nana in redwood trees
and things that grow old together
things that change but never leave

BREAKING & SETTLING

come closer
hear the stillness of my love
I am no longer the same
my yard is turning into dirty apple pie
and things that mattered no longer keep me
desperate and awake
I hear echoes upon mountains of wings
too full for the haunt
I settle into the maple and ash
and sing to a child
a hum like
the white softness of
honeydew melon
a song that proves
the world is breaking
and falling
and settling
over and over again

HEMINGWAY

You came like a hum
like a bird
like a way

rumbling
tumbling
humbling

singing the song of surprise!
eyes wide
A sun!
A son?!
A son!!

burping
chirping
a new dawn is born!
a new mom is born!

like a hum
like a bird
like a way

ringing
singing
bringing

hummm
a hymn!
it's him!
It was you all along

A son!
My sun!

singing
bringing
a new way
of loving
and living

like a hum
like a bird
like a way

my hum
my hem
bringing
singing
a hymn
his way

NOVEMBER

quiet rebellion
to feed and hold my baby
presence in between

Hemingway my love
a hedgehog, a gremlin bird
the light of my life

exhaustion funnel
twilight zone of first few weeks
a blessing of time

god is everywhere
in your breath and your snuggles
in your screams of health

passing through the rite
unconscious, conscious
becoming a family

perfection in flesh
angel nose mouth ears and lips
daddy's perfect ears

blonde in the sunlight
you transform before our eyes
your eyes a deep blue

tiny everything
resist the urge to take in
the bigness of everything

flutters of goddess
the improbable angel
a sun, a moon, stars

fur on precious skin
daddy's mustache on your cheeks
and whiskered kisses

                how were you inside
                and now among us breathing
                now entering every room?

      numbed by lack of sleep
      pencil with no lead no ink
      one must dream to live

      sighing baby bird
      Hemingway our first born son
      snorting little fox

           our world is you
            now we have crossed the great sea
            the side you exist

god answered my prayers
my deepest fears were silenced
my son is healthy

HEART OF THE MOTHER

The heart of the mother beats outside herself
and screams into the dark wind tunnel of prayer,
Unite us once again!
It shrieks like hungry gulls stifled only by a greater need
to survive and hold the heart that breaks at dawn,
knawing at the darkness, groveling on hands and knees to
the milk of life.

The mother sleeps on the surface of night, above all who
rest.
Sounds of need, of pain, of threat, of fear, alert her bones.
On fire she levitates somewhere above the ocean of
dreaming.
There is no greater exhaustion than the body of the
mother.

She rages like a hungry wildfire teetering between
cannibalism and ecstasy.
Silent for fear she might kill the father of her young like a
hungry wild bitch,
waking to the red pulse of love, yearning for more
children in the pack.

The heart of the mother beats outside herself.
It dances with the swirling leaves of mystery.
It perches with the black crow on the cold blue spruce.
It blushes with the morning mountains' alpine glow.

DECEMBER

all I want is sleep
a good eight hours or more
once all in a row

my baby is bliss
and I am too tired to write
to think to be to function

startle and hold tight
the loving baby boo sauce
he holds on for life

no time for wrapping
not for an email or note
and forget cooking

he almost smiled
five weeks, giraffes, and Raffi
I like to eat, eat...

candy-cane muslin
blankets, the tree falls over
bear and fox onesies

don't dare buy a thing
they grow fast and it's over
only for passing

waiting for smiles
savoring the aloneness
cup of liquid morning dreams

Christmas dinner run
nursing baby parking lot
of Heaven Dragon

65

we've come to the end
my counting five and seven
my little one naps

he is here, my child
with a hat and bright blue eyes
sad face makes me cry

first cough, first snow, rain
first Christmas, first everything
first frown, first smile

my angel of God
of Spirit and of Goddess
who loves you? Mama

my sweet angel babe
you were the biggest surprise
all I ever want

to new beginnings
crunching wheel of parenthood
of miracle love

he smiles at my bangs
like his butterflies they fly
and swing in the wind

GOOD MOTHER

Through the window of morning, the round height of your
forehead lights up, a pale autumn lantern above the
shadow of yesterday.
This softest part of you that squeezed through me and
unto earth,
where bones have not yet set,
beats steady and upward toward the vastness of which you
came.

You are the memory I haven't lived. The future I will never see.

I watch you nestle into the crook of my arm, latched for
comfort over milk this early morning. My thinning, break-
ing wisps of hair tickle your cheeks. Smile lines carve the
passing of time into my face.

Miracle who grew inside, how do you fill me more on the outside?
I grind my teeth to not eat you alive, to swallow your dar-
lingness and keep you mine.

Your cries in the night threaten to break me. Your smile at
dawn softens and saves me.

I walk to the kitchen to start the coffee and set you down
in the door frame. Your tiny body crawls toward me, each
hand grasping a toy, you scoot along the floor to be lifted
once more, when just then you spy the open dishwasher,
like a sailor spotting land. Your whole being is sparkling
with aliveness. You quicken your pace. You pull out a sharp
knife. I gasp and take it away.

The good girl lurks in the shadows. Relentless, she stalks,
threatening to grow into the good mother. *You are not wel-
come here good mother.*

The city hasn't awakened, but you have. Like a falcon at daybreak. You open your favorite drawer and search for the largest, heaviest bowl you can find and grab it and throw it behind you as far as you can, you continue until there is nothing left to throw. Only then do you move on to the dog bowl.

I make a bagel with cream cheese and turn on the tv. *You are not welcome here good mother.*

Your love is a universe in and of itself.

Who knew I would have to give so much to get everything I've ever wanted.

BUT THE JOY

I love how you shove food in your mouth with the back
of your hand.

How you are scared of goats.

How you pull at your ear when you nurse

and laugh every time I eat your toes.

I love how you grab anything I put in my hand.

How you sit. How you stand.

I love how you look like an alien in the tub.

How you say hello to every pup.

How you drum and bang things and laugh and smile at
fans.

How you scream for waffles and chew on your hands.

I love how you hum and say uh-oh on the boob.

You are absolutely ridiculous.

I love you.

WHEN IT HURTS

My body rises at dawn, a soft, broken, saddened thing.

A hundred unfinished poems, a lingering argument, a teething child, an aging dog.

When will I sleep again?

I wander down the road of the mother and come to the daily crossroads. Resentment, revenge, forgiveness, amnesia, or distraction?

Today, distraction. *Too tired for revenge.*

Where do all these leaves go that gather in speckled pools? Are they carried off in November winds? Or are they buried beneath the first autumn snow?

I wade through crisp yellow and gold, I crinkle away all the advice I was told.

"When you breastfeed the weight melts right off."

I eat to make more milk.

"You'll never get your pre-baby social life back."

I was over my old life, that's why I had a baby.

"You can breathe through your labor with a support team."

Have you ever tried having an orgasm in front of people?

I spy a plum red tree.

How beautiful you are to me.
Your changing, it is just as deep.
Not only in meadows near snowcapped peaks,
but in parking lots and decrepit streets.
How much more beautiful you are to me
in places beauty is not supposed to be.

A WISH

let us not forget
you were born deep within a Spirit place

a prayer
on the heart of a fish
in a pond on a mountain
in the spring of the soul
a prayer never far away
a wish

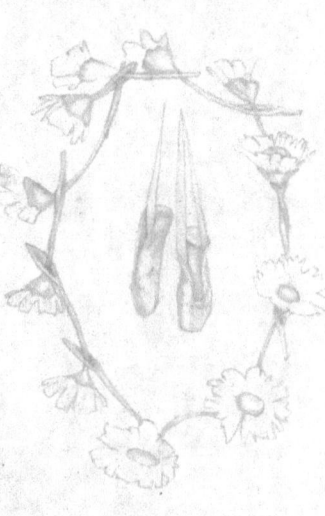

on the lips of a girl
in a house on a hill
in the forest of winter
a wish she dared to make

a leap
of a lion in the grass
on a hunt in a famine
every leap a leap of faith

let us not forget
you were born at the dawn of age

BECAUSE MOTHER IS ALSO A VERB

Staring out at the leaves still barely hanging on, snow coming down in soft wisps, I think to myself...
What am I supposed to do with this baby all alone on a snowy day like today?

Mother.

Mother?

Mother.

What do you mean mother? I can't take him outside, its freezing, snowing, and he has a runny nose and a cough. My house is 1,000 square feet and his grandmas are very far away. I'm bored and lonely and sad.

So mother.

But what does mother mean?

Live.

But I don't know how to live.

You do. If you were a little girl and you had all the freedoms you have now, a car, a home, a kitchen to yourself, what would you do?

I suppose I would find ways to have fun, or try to make something, or try and find friends to play with.

So do that.

But how do I do that with a baby?

When you live he learns to live. When you have fun he might just have fun.

Fun seems so far away.

It is closer than you think.

So mothering is not keeping your child entertained all day?

No.

So mothering is not coming up with a ton of fun things for your child to do?

No.

So mothering is living?

Perhaps.

It is taking a cold, snowy, lonely day like today and living it well?

Yes, living it as well as you can.

Living it and showing him how. With him.

Yes.

So mothering is getting up, getting dressed, brushing my teeth, getting myself some water, making myself some food, and living each day as well as I can?

Perhaps.

Perhaps.

74

WHEREVER I GO

wherever I go you go little moon
wherever I go you go
mountain high
valley low
wherever I go you go

wherever I go you go little one
wherever I go you go
summer sun
winter snow
wherever I go you go

wherever I go you go little moon
wherever I go you go
day or night
wrong or right
wherever I go you go

drum
squirm
punch and roll
wherever I go you go

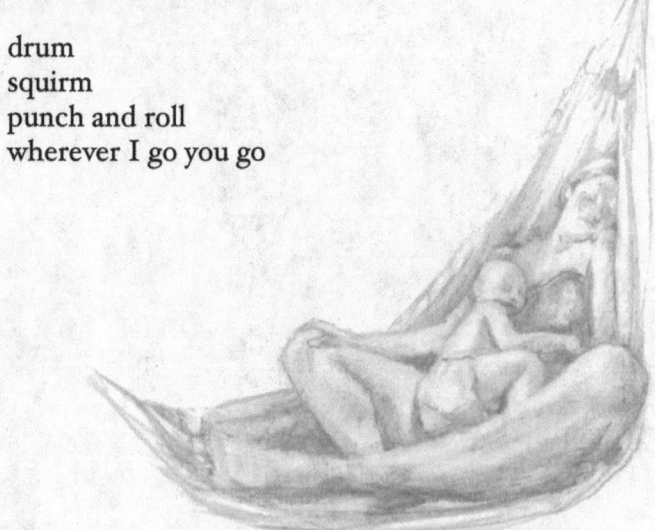

HOME

The city is always prettiest after rain
And what the rain could never wash away
I will clean by hand
clean by hand
clean by hand
I will rewrite every story told too many times
with my ballpoint pen
clean by hand
clean by hand
And what the rain could never wash away
I will clean by hand

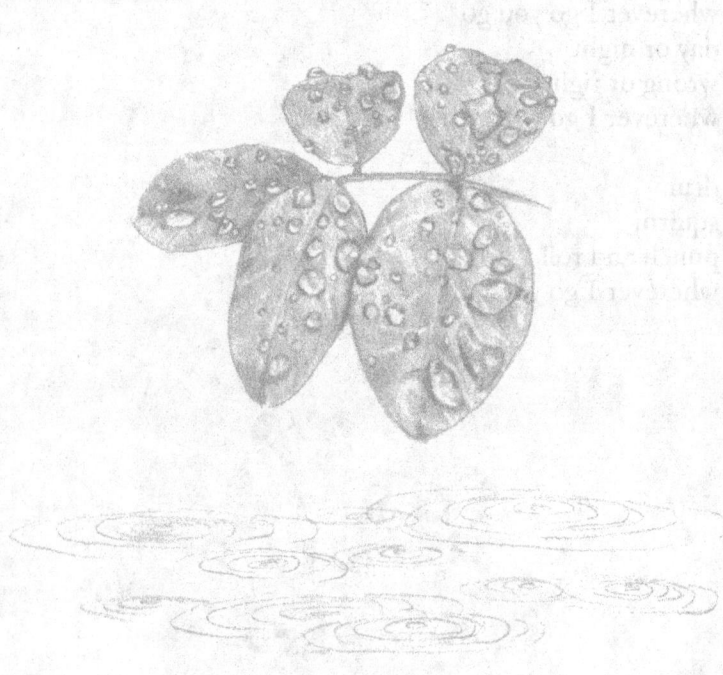

ACKNOWLEDGMENTS

Thank you, Jess, for your remarkable free spirit that soars through your hand and onto these pages and makes these words come to life. I love your art, laughing and making things with you.

Thank you to my beta readers and editors, Teresa, Nancy, Tom, and Nate. Your sharp eyes and thoughtful comments improved this book greatly.

Thank you, Randy Port, for your indomitable faith in my art. Thank you for your encouraging words and the endless supply of macadamia nut fuel you provide for my family. Your thoughtfulness has carried me forward in hard times.

Thank you, Corey and Claudia, for always encouraging my voice as a singer and as a writer. Thank you for giving me a place to go when I am most alone, and for teaching me about friendship and family.

Thank you, Katie, for our many conversations about all the important and hard to articulate things in life, my fearless sister on this path of words and music, I find strength in you.

Thank you, Alli, for your unwavering check-ins throughout my pregnancy, and your unconditional love and dedication to everyone in your life, including me. I am so lucky to call you my best friend.

Thank you, Rachael, for loving my family through it all, and for our artist dates. You remind me that art is also for me to receive.

Thank you, Tom & Currie, for opening your arms to me as my Colorado family. You give me hope and courage, and my life is brighter and bolder because of you.

Thank you, Mom, "Nana", for graciously and joyfully taking care of little Hemingway, giving me time and space to complete this book.

And finally, thank you, Daniel, for being my best friend and for always believing in me. You are my forever love and my Gemini, mountain-man, muse.

ABOUT THE AUTHOR

Carolyn Hunter is a singer, songwriter, and poet. She has published two collections of poetry, *Photographic Memory Camera* and *After Rain*. After a decade of touring in the indie, folk and pop music scenes, Hunter now spends her days writing and rediscovering the world through motherhood. She lives in Colorado with her husband, son, and dog.

carolynhunter.com
Instagram | @carolyn_in_fairyland

ABOUT THE ILLUSTRATOR

Jessica Bernstein is an artist from Lake Tahoe, California. As a painter, illustrator, and animator, she draws from the intricate patterns of nature and the often-overlooked beauty of everyday life. She is an accomplished figure painter known for capturing the female form in its most relaxed, yet empowered, state. Bernstein spends her time skiing, connecting to the natural world, and infusing magic into the ordinary.

Instagram | @jssiegrl

Carolyn and Jessica met backstage at Sawtooth Valley Gathering music festival in Stanley, Idaho. They became instant soul sisters when they found in one another a shared sense of humor and vulnerability, a perspective of laughing through mishaps, and a love of music, art, mischief, dancing, and friendship.

www.ingramcontent.com/pod-product-compliance
Lightning Source LLC
Chambersburg PA
CBHW011239120626
46549CB00009B/3343